I0150731

Meet Me Beyond the Point of No Return

Love Poems
By Stacey Morgenstern

*To my chosen family
whom I love, epically.*

Cover Illustration: LiYana Silver
Book Design: Susan Lee

Printed by CreateSpace, An Amazon.com Company
Available from Amazon.com, CreateSpace.com, and other retail outlets
©2014 Stacey Morgenstern. All rights reserved.

Special thanks to:

Liyana Silver and Nathan Patmor for being a stand for my Desires (incessantly!) and for teaching me to make each moment more pleasurable than the last. You have taught me to live and love with no withholds. I bow in gratitude for how you've changed my life.

Wendy Kay Yalom Photography for helping me fall in love with myself and showing me so exquisitely what it looks like when I embody Yes. Susan Lee for being the tango mistress of layout and design. Without you this would still be a word document on my desktop. Liyana Silver for the gorgeous cover art! I am in awe of your many talents.

Jena La Flamme for teaching me the Intimate Decline. Without your Goddessing I would not have felt safe to flaunt beauty so freely. Bryan Franklin and Jennifer Russell for loving words as much as I do and always believing the possibilities in my impossibles. Sonya Stewart for exponentially increasing the Love in our orbit. Sergio Lialin for making me feel so graceful. Kate Niebauer for kindling so much inspiration with the depth of your expression. Ariana Hall for guiding me back to the Muse. Ilya Jacobson for being my poet lover and pirate. Kala Wright for being One of Those She's. Michael Ellsberg for reminding me that every writer needs story space.

The Women of the Mistressmind: Liyana Silver, Nisha Moodley, Jena La Flamme, Kc Baker, Ali Shanti, Jennifer Russell, and Wendy Yalom. Without you, I'd wither.

The shall-not-be-named benefactors who made this book possible. I am humbled by your constant generosity. My Oracle thanks you.

Skyla Zoe Kellett for being my greatest teacher. I am forever grateful to be in the way of your Love.

Gregory Kellett for leading me back Home to my senses again and again and again. Because of you, I am never lost.

Beyond The Point Of No Return

Will you go there with me, love,
beyond the point of no return?

They say no one has ever come back
from that place

"I bet it's an epic adventure," you said,
squeezing my hand in that way that means I love you

And together we took a blind step into the unknown

Beyond.

Decant Your Turn On

Flirting is the
whole body experience
of loving yourself,
being amused
by the world around you,
and letting that
overflow to others,
without agenda.

It's beautifying,
beguiling,
mesmerizing,
empowering,
and enriching.

It can be done by anyone
at any age and
it's FREE.

If you want access
to the
Infinite Leaking Barrel of Life Force,
decant your turn on and
let it spill over.

Soon we will all be drunk on
self-love and
dancing to the soundtrack of
God's orgasmic anthem:
"Yes! Yes! Yes!"

Foreplay between the Intellexual and the Lover

"Kiss me your words…" she said.
"One kiss is all I want."

The desire was palpable
In the space between them.

It's the touch that's already touching
Before the touch.

"Come here and take off your clothes,"
He commanded tenderly.

She moaned his request
And stepped closer…
Tilting her chin to gaze up
At this beautiful man.

"One kiss is all I want." she smiled coyly.

He could feel her sweet breath on his neck
A sultry spell
That made his mouth water.

The space between them was almost unbearable
But he knew better
Than to rush the moment.

With his deep husky voice he groaned,
"Where shall I kiss you, my love?"

Even though he already knew the spot that drove her crazy,
He wanted to hear her speak it aloud
A broadcast of her desire

Drunk on his words
Her clothes fell off

"Here, please." She pleaded, sweeping her hair to one side
Revealing her weakness to him.

Anticipation took her bow
And silkily slipped away

Desire coalesced
The space between dissolved

This
in which
there is no more
You or I.

Bare Essentials

Come here and take off your clothes.
Where we're going, you won't be needing them.

Wants Untold

Let's hide under the covers
and tell each other wants untold.

Voluntary Epic Love Inception

The instant you so gallantly

held open the door to your heart
and invited me to climb inside and grow…

I dove in head over heels.

"I Love You"
is a threesome so erotic,
the words never tire of their
coupling.

I Love To Be Loved By You

I love you for loving me in all the ways that
I love to be loved by you

And marvel that this happens to be
the way that you love to love me too.

Sleep me from this wakefulness

I lay awake
wishing
you would come
lay your naked skin
upon mine and
kiss away the insomnia
caused by my
dreaming awake about
your naked skin
upon mine.

One Of Those She's

She is one of those SHE'S...

When she walks into a room
Everyone turns to admire
Her hair - Soft curls framing sloped cheekbones
Her crimson lips - Naturally the shape most women pay money to pencil in
Brown eyes that drink you in and warm your soul
And of course a body that just won't quit

She is one of those SHE'S

When she speaks it's poetry
When she reads you're dying to know what she is reading
because it could be about love, sex, hindu gods, jewelry making or pleidians...

When she makes tea, she makes it special
For herself
because she loves she

She is one of those SHE'S

She adorns herself like a goddess
And leaves a trail of beauty in every room
She loves all the way this one
An ecstatic slow dance that knows no withholds
She is one of those SHE's

And perhaps her greatest unnamed gift of all
When I am with her
I love me

What do they call that? People ask.
They call that Ka-Love. And it's transferred
from one being to the next and the next and the next
even long after we're gone.

Epic love, the kind that is healing the world
Was born from the open heart
Of women like SHE.

The Crane Game

Out of 7,210,324,613 people, I choose you.

Second Skin

Can I be your favorite dress
so I can hug you all the time?

You Crazy Fool You - Hardy Harr Harr

Some called me crazy when I shouted your name
over and over again from the rooftops.

"I'm not crazy," I told them, "I'm just a fool for your love.
If that's your definition of crazy, then I am inclined to agree!"
I exclaim slap-happily double quoting myself.

Surrendered

"I claim this spot."
She declared,
standing on her
tippy toes
tugging his hair
and planting
her teeth
into the slope of
his neck.

He gasped as his armor
crashed to the floor

Never to be worn
again in
her presence.

For Just A Moment

He put his hand
on the small of
my back
as I stood
working at the
kitchen counter
so we could
stand close,
breathing
together
for just
a moment.

As Is... No Returns

Even though I'm missing buttons and
keep dragging loose threads around…

Even though I'm impossible to iron or
fit in a box…

Even though I'm pilly from life's wears and tears…

Even though there's a small hole in the chest
where the cold gets in…

Even though my tag says,
"As Is… No Returns."

Would you still take me home with you
wherever you go?

"I can't leave without this one."
You tell the young salesgirl as you plug
the hole in my chest with your long, graceful finger.

"Even though---?" she started, but he immediately cut her off.
"Because." he insisted firmly.

The young salesgirl shrugged,
"Suit yourself, sir, but just so you know
this one is As Is... No Returns."

Her ignored her, fondly inspecting all of my
Even though's...

And for the first time in a long time
my heart felt warm.

Two Heads Giggling in the Spring Grass

When I call out shapes
and animals in the clouds
you never give up before
you see what I see.

I point and paint the sky with
translucent ink, watching the clouds
gently move in response.

Then there's the exact moment
when you finally see
with crystal clarity
that albino rhineroceros
eating giant cotton candy

And we laugh and fall in love
all over again.

I wonder if the clouds play the
same game and what shape they
would make of you and me,
two heads
giggling in the spring grass.

Indent

So many nights
I have reached
across
the bed
into
the empty space
you
should be filling.

The Present

This morning I woke up and there was a present
sleeping next to me.

I unwrapped it and found epic love.

The Skirt

Today I went shopping.
Everywhere I went,
I thought of you.

Fingering the soft fabrics
in a store where
everything is much too expensive,
I saw a long
black skirt
with a
playful ruffle
at the bottom.

Nothing extraordinarily special, but I was
anxious to feel
the ruffle
against
my bare ankles
and
imagine
your lips
brushing against
my skin.

I grabbed
the smallest one so it would
hug my ass
the way you do when I am on top
of you.

I end up buying
that way too expensive skirt
because it gives me
the sensational feeling
of being touched
by you.

I laugh
under my breath
as the saleswoman tells me
how lovely it is and all I am thinking is
I can't wait to wear
my Way-Too-Expensive-Skirt
so I can see it
crumpled on
your floor.

Love Times Infinity

Forever isn't as long as I'd hoped
to spend with you, but I'll take it
if you'll have me.

Converse

The moonlight would be nothing
without the darkness
to illuminate it.

You Make Me Want To Sin

"You're fun." she said innocently.
"I know." he grinned wickedly.

Birthday Poem

On this day you came into this world as you.

Embracing you joyfully in her arms you're mother
whispered lovingly in your ear, "So glad you are.
So glad you are."

And you understood.

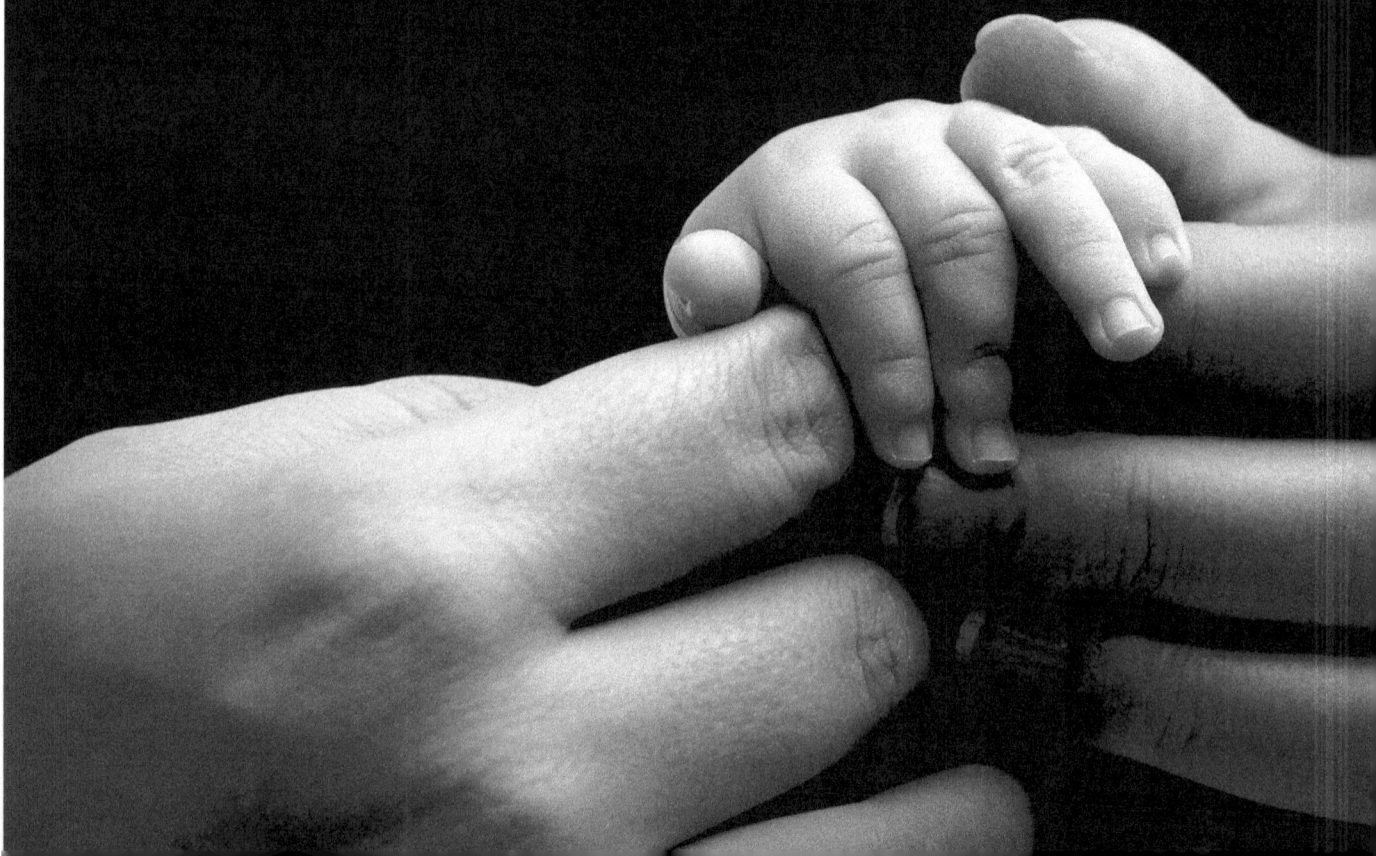

Magic Trick

"If we shut our eyes we will become instantly invisible, together."

Everything feels like magic when I'm with you.

Everything Good

To me you're the moon, lighting my way through dark nights.
To me you're the sun that wakes me up everyday.
To me you're the warm when I'm cold.
To me you're everything good
All at once.

La Flamme

May
Love's desire
be the Holy Fire
that lights
the Way
inside
your heart.

Wild Poetess On The Loose

"What is it?" the boy wondered curiously. "Is it some kind of lioness?"

The man replied unable to take his eyes off her, "That, my boy, is a wild poetess on the loose!"

"Should we catch her and put her in a cage so she'll never leave us?"

"Oh no, son. That would be our own suicide."

The man and the boy watched the wild poetess in awe for she kept changing before their eyes... each time a stunning revelation, discovering her beauty as if for the very first time.

"There are many wild poetesses, my son, and they have been caged far too long, but I've heard rumors they are on the loose in droves once again."

"Oh goodie! Can we get more of whatever sets them free and plant fields of it so this never happens again? Please, dad, we have to!"

"Just take notice of how each one loves to be loved.
Then simply love her and she'll free herself."

"Oh. I'll need training in that." said the boy.

The man sighed and smiled proudly,
squeezing the boy close and feeling
hopeful again.

Photo by: Wendy K Yalom

I Feel Loved When

I feel loved when…

you serve me dinner on beautiful plates.
you fold my laundry.
you kiss that spot on my neck.
you rub my feet.
you read me poetry.
you invite me into an experience.
you surprise me with flowers and love notes.
you make me a smoothie when i have a busy morning.
you tell me a secret.
you so lovingly let me know where I can grow.
you remind me that I am awesome when i forget.
you refill my coffee.

you clean my house after a party.

you bring me water when I'm thirsty in bed so i don't have to get up.
you let me put my cold hands on your warm body.
i enter the room and you are excited to see me.

you alleviate the frustration of not being able to find the thing I want by providing the very thing I'm looking for.

you itch my scratch and scratch my itch.
you kinestetically express your pleasure of experiencing me.
you say, "I love what you just said!"

you are relaxed, embodied, wild and free in my presence.
you leave me a comment on facebook.
you ask, "how may I love you today?"

you patiently tease the orgasm out of me with your feather like touch.

you let me sleep in.
you pleasurably do the things that are not pleasurable for me.

you share a favorite piece of music.
you teach me something new.
you love me with your eyes in a way that renders words superfluous.

you tuck me in.
your skin deliberately makes contact with mine in the middle of the night.

you investigate my desires and then covertly conspire a reality where my desires are what's I'm experiencing.

you receive my love.

I feel
Loved.

Nothing Shall Be Forbidden in Epic Love

"Have I ever told you how much I deeply love you?" he said tenderly with dazzling eyes that reflected his awe of her beauty.

And just like that she opened like a morning glory.

"Have I ever told you how much I love to hold you in my mouth?" she replied mischievously and dropped to her knees, eyes locked with his.

He could do nothing more than surrender, which was everything.

And just like that nothing was forbidden between them.

God's Heartbreak

When all Men
had been
slain

And there were
no more arms
to hug
the hurt away

I asked God
why she
suited them in armor
and gave them
arrows
to spear
each others
hearts

"Amor," She
choked back tears,
"Not armor."

God looked
at me with a
broken heart

Why didn't
anyone ask
this sooner?

It's impossible to
contemplate
God's heartache
over this.

Lusty Listening

My body has unsay-able things to
tell your body.

Show me your lustening and I will
bare my secrets.

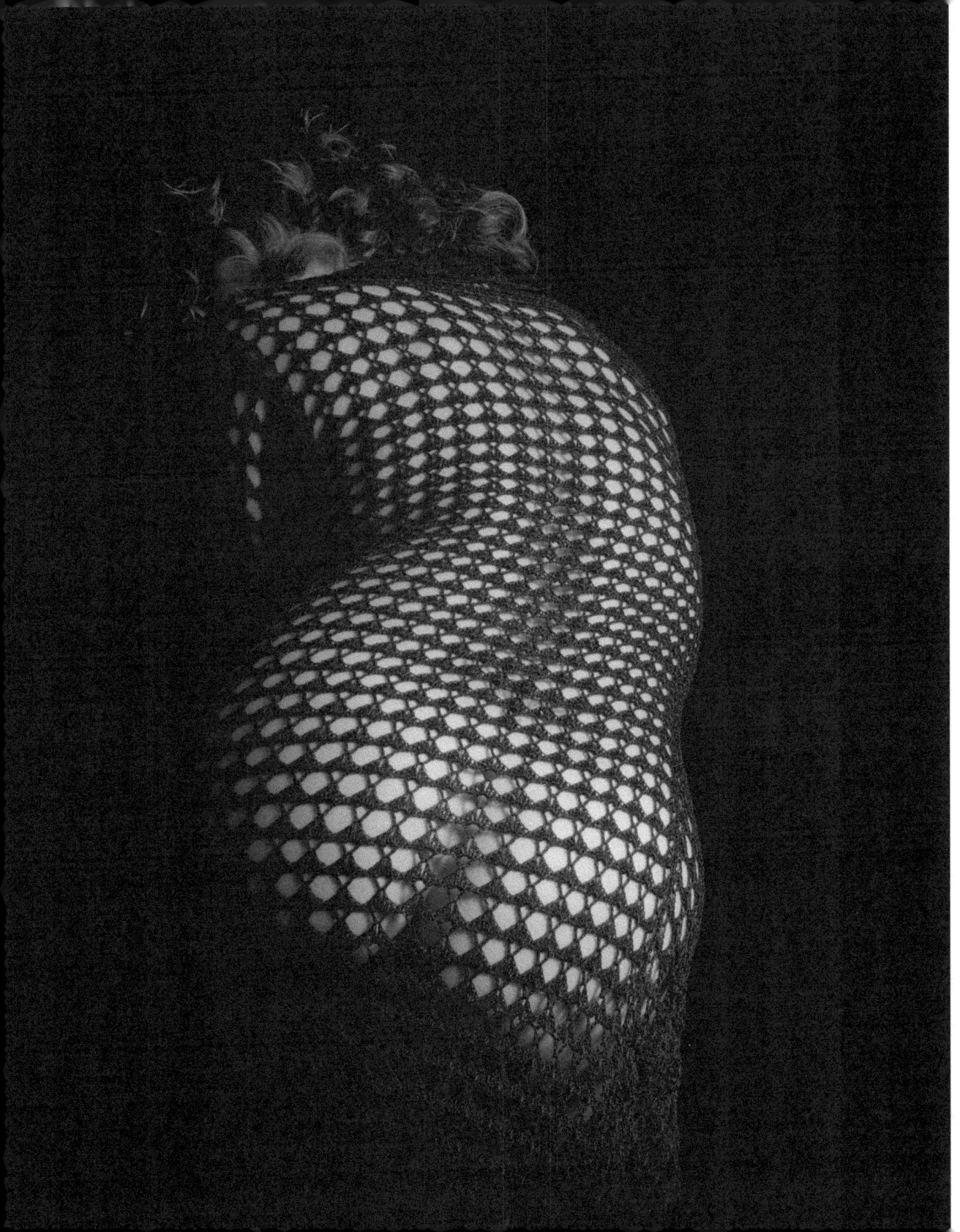

Panoramic Homecoming

He spotted her in baggage claim
Smiling at the sight of her
As she approached.

He opened his arms
Heart on the front line
Unprotected, unshielded
Offering her the whole wide world.

So much told, but unspoken in this gesture.
"Welcome home, love." He said.

She pressed herself fully against his chest
Willing him to coil his arms tightly around her
And hug the air out of her lungs
So she could get closer by exhaling just a little more.

"Have I told you yet today how much I love you?"
He whispered tenderly.

"Not yet," she grinned adoringly.

And just like all the seemingly first times before
She gave herself to his 360 degree warm embrace
And felt completely and utterly
Received.

What they treasured most about being apart
Was the way Life always brought them back together
Like the Universe celebrating its own
Panoramic Homecoming.

The Point Of No Return

You once said
we were
approaching
the point
of no return…

"I am already there,"
I smiled
and kissed
your mouth
from
beyond.

Urgency

A lifetime passes in the time it takes
to unbuckle your buckle
when clothes are suddenly excessive
and getting rid of them is urgent.

Pilot

He reads me
like a map
and
takes me
exactly
where
I
want
to
go.

Find Yourself

Do you find yourself in my poetry?
Promise me you'll never leave the premises.

Storylines

Time etches on the face of my beloved
I trace each line and relive his story,
Our story.

For I knew this face when it was a
boyish untouched canvas.

Sometimes I wake up in the middle of the night
and catch him smiling ever so slightly in his sleep,
two indents outlining each side of his mouth,
quoting his peaceful grin.

Some call them wrinkles
I call them storylines
To me, his face is like art
You can look at it everyday for the rest of your life
And always see something new

Today I noticed that I love him more than I did yesterday
And not as much as I will tomorrow
Or 50 years after that

Because the etchings will keep telling
The story of Our love
And that is a subject
I will never grow weary of.

The Curve

He follows the curve
of her hip and
always finds
his way
home.

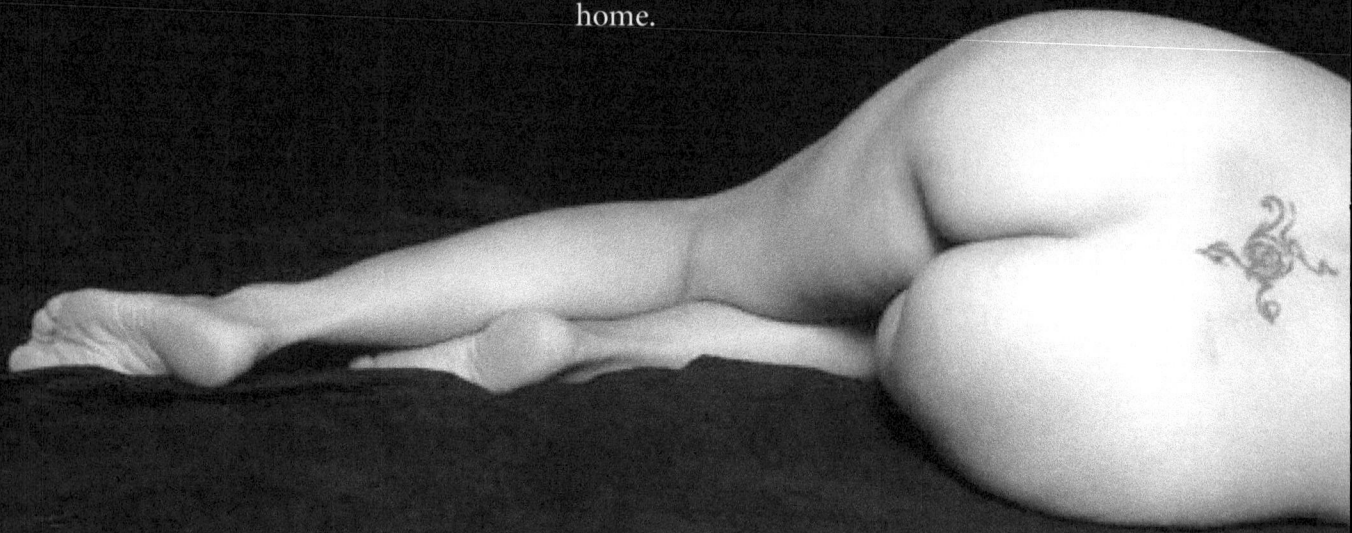

Beauty Mark

Perfectionism bit me today
and left an itchy, infectious, ugly wound.

I really wanted to scratch it, but I know that only
makes it worse.

So I looked again with fresh eyes
at the things that seemed so indelibly flawed
and found what was perfect already.

It turns out
the itchy, infectious, ugly wound is
a beauty mark.

InsomniART

I keep choosing Poetry over sleep.
Poetry IS that good in bed.

Simultaneous Orgasm

So intimate that our hearts synch;
and for just this one, logic defying moment
it seems that we share one heart between I and you.

My Beloved Novelty

From the first time
I met you
I knew I would know you

because it seemed
like I always had.

Now I'm spending my life
getting to know you
like I never did.

Everyday I discover something
that makes you new
One thousand times a day
I think I just fell in love with you

Some couples tell me they get bored and flee.
"It happens every 18 months."
They claim faithfully.

I wonder how soon after meeting they
start the breakup countdown?

Ticking time bomb
Maddening murderous monotony
Misfortune teller of love's fatality

When does a relationship start to feel stale?

It's when two people stop discovering what
they love about each other and bale.

I'm convinced the secret to my seemingly
inextinguishable love

Is to be one of many matches
that sparks the fire
that stokes
an unpredictable you

You are
separately becoming
and that's what makes you
everlastingly new
to me.

My beloved novelty.

Where Does The Love Go?

It's draining for a man
when a woman doesn't
receive.

It's draining for
the woman too.

I wonder sometimes,
Where does all that Love go?

Endearingly Egotistical

i have written you countless love poems
and i will write you thousands more

people credit me with me having a gift
but they always forget to credit you too.

is it terribly selfish and egotistical that i can't stop
wondering what it would be like to be you
who inspire so many love poems from me?

if I told you I was embarrassed by this confession
would you find me endearlingly humble?

Hide-n-Seek

May the
Love
that is
hunting You
find your
hiding spot.

Going Down

Your turn on is my compass.
Heading south now.

Savor This

I am an epic love poem
begging you to read me
and say mmmm.

The Magic of You

Smiling mischievously pondering all the ways you melt me
and grateful that I don't have to choose which one I like best
because i like them all the best

This is the magic of you

It always feels like my favorite kiss
my favorite stroke
my favorite moment

Somehow this comes as a surprise
because just before my favorite moment I will have forgotten
so that I might fall in love with you
(again)

And it's effortless

This is the magic of you.

Deep Breaths Are Inspirations

Belly's touching you hug all the breath out of my body until it is completely empty and fill the hollow space with your inspiration.

You won't admit it, but I think that might be your covert strategy for bellowing all this epic love poetry into me.

Desire is My Lover

Desire is my lover
She seeks to push the edges
in the places where I have drawn
a line in the sand that says,
"This is where I will not go. This is what I will not risk."

Desire petitions to be noticed
Yearns to fulfill my every wish

"How may I make this moment
more pleasurable?" She croons
earnestly into the maddening
precipice of Refusing-to-Receive.

"Shhhh." I reply bluntly.
"Stay quiet until I tell you
it's safe to come out.
Don't you get it?
We can't be together now.
I'm not good enough
for you yet."

I clamp down on Desire
like a heavy heart
weighting an overstuffed suitcase of
intractable silk garments

Desire is my lover
But I locked her up in a sealed glass fortress
at my own Please Touch Museum
so I would be tortured by the pain of a beauty
I could not allow myself
to enjoy

Desire is my lover
I cheated on her with all the others
Running from her rich invitations into
the arms of Disappointment, Guilt, Shame,
Scarcity, Self-loathing and Despair.

Yes, I fuck them ALL,
but Desire is my lover.

Lover, will you forgive me for denying you all this time?
Let's get undressed.
I have a request.

If You Were The Sun

If you were the sun
I'd be happy to be blinded
by you
if it meant I'd
be filled
with your light.

Epic Love in Small Things

A loose tendril of hair fell
across her face.
She smiled adoringly
as his fingers
brushed her
soft cheek,
hooking the curl back
behind her ear.

No one could tell
which one of them
took greater pleasure
in this simple exchange.

The Swell

Caress my sandy beaches with your
salty kisses
Soft ripples teasing, pleasing,
receding
into an Ocean of desire.
Rising tide
I'm dizzy with wonder
the swell
of your love tsunami
casts a spell
I am already under.
Storm my castle
splash, crash,
pent-up longings
unloosed at last.
Take me, Ocean
on your ride.
Part my legs,
Open My Pride!
Lick me from this coast
we'll set sail,
you and me,
into the Great Mystery,
Eternally

Exposed

Open...
Close.
Open!

"Button your coat! It's cold outside."

Close.
Open...

"Honey, you need a coat to go out-
side. You'll freeze to death!"

Close.
Open... reveal!
Revel.
Rebel.
Wrestle.
A little more... Yes

Say hello to that stranger walking his
dog.

"Don't talk to strangers dear."
Close.

Open?

He says hello back and grins.
He's not scary afterall.

It's joyfully dangerous and not as
cold as she thought
Out of the house

Exposed

We Were Strangers Too Once

I thought I saw you
Smiling knowingly at me through the crowd
So familiar
That gaze
Like when we were lovers
And knew all of each others secrets

Through the crowd
We lived out all our silly fantasies

Like learning to tango
And say "I love you" in a 100 different languages
Starting a food fight in a fancy restaurant
Drinking wine straight from the barrel and
Fucking in the self-help section of the public library

The wind made my eyes tear
I blinked
And when I looked up at you
Through wet lashes
You had faded into the crowd
A sea of strangers
Huddled against the cold

I turned and wondered
If it really was you after all

We were strangers too once

Perhaps that's what's so familiar
About seeing you
In a crowd.

Naked Yes

Breathe her body to open,
moment by moment,
kiss by kiss.

When she trusts your touch,
her skin will reach
achingly
for your hand.

This wait is so worth it.
The patient man will discover
heaven on earth

With every reach
her heart opens.

With every touch
her desire builds.

The divine ache
to be filled.

The thirst
before the quench.

Her defenseless
Naked
YES.

Everywhere You Go

I lost my heart inside a red balloon
the wind
carried me across the world
like a tiny boat that
sails towards that dock
of yours waiting for me
I was brave
but worn
when you found me
deflated at your footstep
with barely any life
left in me
broken,
but beautiful still
in your eyes
you covered my mouth with your
soft lips
and gave me your breath
until I was full again

How quickly I was smitten
with the way you
tangled your fingers
tightly through mine
and proudly bounced down the street
with your prized red balloon
wanting nothing more
in the world than
to carry my heart
everywhere
you go.

Dandelion Wishes

Pray tell child, what are you wishing for?
I offer you the world.

With love,
Mama.

Silly Love

If you are adorable, adoration will come to you
because adoration likes to go where adorable is.

Love
is the
simplest answer
to any question
that
begins with
Why?

Meet Me There in 5

The race of my heart
when I find you
staring
directly at me
from across a crowded room
with a mischievous smirk
on your distracting lips.

Where do you take me in that moment?

I'll meet you there in 5.

Time Travel

I wish here was there faster or there was here.
I'm hurrying as fast as I can, my love, so
I can take my time with you.

JFK - SFO

Let The Cold Come Now

You shook the walls I built
Screamed louder than the rebellious
voices inside
Told them that you loved me
(Despite their persistent protest)

You marveled at my flaws
Planted kisses like seeds
All across my skin
So that I might grow to love me
The way you love me

You with your skeleton key
Druid of my heart
Sorcerer of Love
I was starving in the middle of a Feast
And didn't even know it.

Your hands
Are made from things
We all have trouble believing

When I saw myself
through your eyes
I thought you *must* be dreaming

I remember the instant
So precisely and perfectly
When it dawned on me
That you were not dreaming at all
But WIDE AWAKE!

That was the day I ran out of stories
And started to believe

That's the day all the barriers
I had built came
Tumbling down

That's the day epic love was born
The Resistance was finally over
We danced naked in the streets
Nothing left to hide.

Let the cold come now
There's no one better than you
To warm me up.

Home Grown

I promise
to keep
clearing the weeds
so there will
always be room
in the garden
of my heart
for you
to grow.

Ineffable

I am a thesaurus
composed
of ten thousand ways
to describe
the miracle of
you

And still,
it's ineffable.

Heavenly Kisses

Raindrops
falling from the sky
collect on my tongue

Close your eyes
and part your lips

So that I may quench
your thirst
with heaven's moist kiss.

If I Died

If I died I'd like to come back as
your sheets, so I could wrap myself
around you when you're naked.

Humanity's Salve

Smiling women are humanity's salve.
Spark it and be healed.

Eden's Jewel Thief

in
the
garden
the
tickle
of your
warm breath
on
my neck
beckons me
to tilt my face
towards the
midnight sky

moon beams above
a black blanket quickly
sheaths her
alabaster beauty

one last crescent sliver
illuminating glimpse
before the
blinding shadow
of the
lunar eclipse

drunk on Tuberose and Gardenia's night bloom
you steal the last light of the
sapphire moon
from my
honeysuckle lips
Eden's jewel thief, taste my sweet kiss
before we both disappear
in the dark

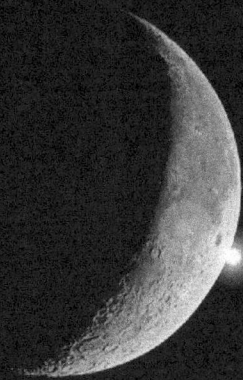

Lodestar

No matter how dark it gets over here,
promise me you will shine your light
so I can always find my way home.

It's That Kind Of I Love You

I knew from the moment
you looked into my eyes
and said you loved me,
truly loved me…
that any unbearable would
be bearable
because it suddenly dawns on me that all that I lack
has been living inside of you all this time

It's that kind of I love you
that makes me smush
my body against yours
inviting you to zipper me up
in your straightjacket embrace
squeeze the air out of my lungs
as if we could be closer still by exhaling just a little bit more

It's that kind of I love you like I've never loved anyone,
that feels like more than I deserve

It's that kind of I love you that makes me want to burn
in your fire knowing I will probably never heal from this

It's that kind of I love you that means if I die
you're the one that has to know
because that matters somehow

It's that kind of I love you that rips the doors off the hinges
of every basement of my being that once hung a sign screaming, "keep out!"

It's that kind of I love you where nothing shall be forbidden
between us

It's the kind of I love you that's merely an appetizer to a 9-course meal
which is way more than I know how to receive but I'm willing to learn

It's that kind of I love you where time collapses
and no thought remains
except that I want your mouth on mine
And so I kissed you with my everything in an effort to say
I love you in your language

And you drank me in and somehow the more you drank
the more full I was

I knew from that moment that beyond the point of no return was to be
the place we were pushing off of
from then on.

Becoming

Weathering
the rocky seas.
Clutching
my chosen gripes.
I am lost
in the storm.
It feels
like I'm drowning.

Be patient with me, love.
I am in
the process of
becoming
so much
More
than I ever was
before.

Feels Like Home

When I'm with you
It feels beautiful being me.

I guess that's why
Everywhere you are
Feels like Home.

www.ingramcontent.com/pod-product-compliance
Lightning Source LLC
LaVergne TN
LVHW061227060426
835509LV00012B/1458

9 780099 147230 7